Thriver's Quest

healing life's traumas to bring out your best

poems

by

M.E. Hart

Dean,

Thank you for what
you do!
with gratitude.

Hart

ISBN 978-1-61846-055-4

Cover Design: MJ Vilardi

Inquiries can be made at info@thriversquest.com

This is a work for your personal use and nothing within constitutes medical or legal advice. The intent of the author is to help you in your quest for personal well-being. If you are receiving treatment, the author supports your efforts and suggests that you follow the ongoing recommendations, supervision, and care of your certified and trained professional. If you are doing personal research please keep a hotline support phone number close by as you work with this material.

Produced and Distributed By:

Library Partners Press
ZSR Library
Wake Forest University
1834 Wake Forest Road
Winston-Salem, North Carolina 27106

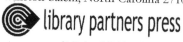 library partners press
a digital publishing imprint

www.librarypartnerspress.org

Manufactured in the United States of America

Experience: the most brutal of teachers.

But you learn,

my God do you learn.

– C. S. Lewis

Preface – Author's Note – Open Letter to Thrivers in Process

TABLE OF CONTENTS

Final Note: Respect your unique journey through life.

For some people, a few of these poems might create mild to strong emotional triggers due to some similarities in your experiences.

Please take care of yourself if emotional triggers happen. Have a trusted hotline number available as you work through this book.

Be gentle with yourself and good luck on your healing journey.

Preface

We all face challenges just living life. I am thriving after facing some of life's steepest challenges. I imagine you have your personal list of challenges and triumphs, too.

As a little boy, I got the message that the *Strong Silent Type* was the only *real* man. The story goes that real men are supposed to deal with traumas privately. Whether childhood sexual abuse, bullying, racial prejudice, tragic deaths of family and friends, illnesses, violent accidents; everything is to be kept quiet and private.

I, like many little boys, learned this when I was too young to even know what we were being taught. Unconsciously picking up these messages, abused boys, and traumatized men, often begin their healing journey suffering in silence.

I was one of them. Isolating, and simultaneously trying to live up to the myth of the *Strong Silent Type,* was all I knew to do. Many in society have no idea what an overwhelming challenge that can be.

So what's a *man* to do? Answer the call to healing and *Thrive* anyway!

I first spoke publicly about my sexual abuse on Black Entertainment Television in 1990, with two other African American males, and psychotherapist Mike Lew. I broke the silence again, 20 years later, standing with 200 other men in the final season of the Oprah Winfrey Show in 2010.

I want to shine a bright light on - *THRIVING* after surviving sexual assaults, and other life traumas. The poems in this book represent a unique way of telling these stories.

My healing journeys centered around six themes:

1. **Surviving**   4. **Realizing**

2. **Searching**   5. **Healing**

3. **Fighting**   6. **Thriving**

I discovered them through many years of listening to the stories of men and women who were working to heal from sexual abuse.

Listening to their stories, and reading everything I could get my hands on, was my first step in healing. I have learned that many survivors of sexual assault start their journey the same way.

I have used the six themes I discovered in designing this book. Let's take a look at your three options for exploring them.

How to Use This Book

Option 1: You might just want to read and enjoy the poems.

Option 2: You may choose to read the poems, and use them as a starting point to begin writing your own poems based on each theme.

Option 3: You may choose to use these poems in your individual healing work with a therapist; or to share in a group to help its members understand what you are thinking and feeling at a specific point in your healing.

Each poem represents one moment in time on my healing *Thriver's Quest.*

The main work of healing for me included looking at specific thoughts, emotions, feelings, events, and relationships.

Thoughts, and feelings, can seem chaotic when we are at the beginning of our healing journey; so I developed a simple system for writing poems I call: The MiniQuest Writing Process. It is a short version of the Hero's Journey inspired by the work of mythologist Joseph Campbell.

It is a simple focusing tool that can be helpful regardless of how long you have been writing.

The three MiniQuest steps are:

The Call

The Quest

The Return

The **Call** can be a thought, a feeling, a sensation, a dream, a question we ask ourselves, or a question someone asks us, anything really. It is what sparks us to try to understand what's happening in a given moment.

The **Quest** is writing down what we are thinking, feeling, remembering, fantasizing, and imagining as we explore the thoughts, feelings, bodily responses, and actions that catch our attention. Then we spend some time putting what we have discovered into a poetic form that deepens our understanding and healing.

The **Return** is re-visiting our poems to help us understand ourselves better as we have new responses to them. Often, we discover that re-reading our poems helps us make sense of something in our present life.

Bonus: I have included the three MiniQuest steps after each poem in the body of this book. They give examples of how this approach can be used.

Each poem is the outcome of answering a single call to healing and taking imaginative adventures into my internal landscapes.

It is something any of us can do.

These internal journeys help us reconnect to our deepest self and to ultimately rediscover who we are born to be, and what we are born to offer the world.

These poems were inspired by my journeys – and the journeys of the countless men and women I have met – along my ongoing Thriver's Quest.

Personal Note: No names or other identifying factors are presented about the male and female *muses* who inspired some of these poems. I invite you to read them and share them.

To the Thriver's working with professionals I say: *"Use my words as you work to find your own, with the supervision, support, and guidance of your counselor."*

It is important to take care of yourself as you do any healing work.

That is true even when reading these poems.

Whether you are in treatment – or are a family member, friend or ally of someone seeking treatment for trauma – at any point, if you find yourself emotionally triggered and struggling in silence, please stop reading and seek assistance.

You may contact your certified therapist, or call a national hotline, and speak with someone who can help you sort out your thoughts and feelings and to find options for support.

Resources in your community may be found through a simple internet search.

At every turn, please give yourself permission to take care of yourself. You deserve it.

Author's Note

Why Poetry? Because: **A Poem**

---

a poem needs to say
  what a poem needs to say
and a poem needs to say it
  in a poem's own way
and when a poem is spoken
  on any given day
it may change a life forever
  in some small
  or very profound way

life, like a poem

a life needs to say
  what a life needs to say
and a life needs to say it
  in a life's own way
and any given act
  on any given day
may change a life forever
  in some small
  or very profound way

An Open Letter to Thrivers in Process

Dear Thriver To Be:

Regardless of what anyone else says: You matter. Your life matters. You have a right to be here, to live here, and to thrive here.

You are worth the work it takes – struggling to reconnect with just one living soul – to help anchor you. To find someone who can stand as a witness with you. I had pent up horror that I couldn't share with anyone for too many years.

The *Strong Silent Type* is just one way to be a man; and in my experience, it is far from what life is really like as a healthy human being. My journey taught me that we are all unique; and that we have the right to explore all of our complexity to discover who we are born to be.

 Still today, our society constantly sends subtle – and not so subtle – messages that there are some things we, as men, don't talk about. Many in society don't want us to talk about the wounds of our souls, because they would prefer to deny that the events that cause these wounds can even happen.

This social silence – denial and avoidance – reflects a collective level of being uncomfortable with facing tough, dark truths. If we are honest, we would prefer to not have to deal with these issues too.

So when *life* pushes us hard in the direction of healing; when *life* forces us to decide to face what has happened to us; we often must move forward alone, at least for part of the journey.

M.E. Hart   *Thriver's Quest ix*

When that happens, it becomes important to find a way to honor our truths, our growing awareness, our courage, and our strength. The wounded, healing, and painful places within us all deserve our attention.

I found poetry a powerful way to give voice to the voiceless parts of my soul. Poetry also let me present parts of my story in a way that wouldn't overwhelm the people I sought help from.

At first, I wrote poems just to honor my soul, to name pain, to release shame, to give what happened to me names: abuse, attempted soul murder, deep psychological pain.

I also used poetry to carry me through the searching part of the journey; to give voice to healing realizations when they came; to turn them into healing strategies that would lead to living a life where I thrive.

With a lot of work, I moved from suffering in silence to living as a *Silent Thriver*. That is my Thriver's Quest. These poems represent just a few of the moments along the way. I humbly offer them to you, to assist you in your healing.

If a hero's journey is worth making movies about, your thriver's adventures in healing is what life is really about.

It's not just one story, it's not a myth, and you may never see a movie that touches on all the struggles, trials, and triumphs you face.

I just want you to know, you are not alone. There are many of us. We were hurt. We survived. We heal. We thrive.

Give yourself a chance, you can too.

M.E. Hart   *Thriver's Quest x*

Surviving

M.E. Hart

Thriver's Quest 2

Long ago

long ago
  and far away
something happened
  that touches today
if we can't find it
  and set it free
where we are now
  is where we will stay
day, after day, after day
and we're not sure
we can go on this way
there are too many horrors
  in our hearts

we don't know where to start
not at the beginning
  it's just too dark

not in the middle
  we don't know where that is
not at the end
  we haven't made it there yet

there are too many horrors
  in our hearts

we don't know what else to say
  we don't know where to start

Long Ago MiniQuest

The Call
At the beginning of our healing process we don't know how to get a handle on the feelings and sensations that seem to come out of nowhere. They well up inside. They leak into situations in ways we don't understand. They seem to be out of our control. It is disturbing, confusing, and irritating.

The Quest
The first question is, "Where to start to understand what's happening to us?" The first answer we get is, "We don't know where to start." We don't know where to start because we think there are too many horrors to deal with. Exploring the *idea* of not knowing where to start *is the place to start*.

The Return
When I return to this poem it confirms, "Yep that's what it felt like at the beginning of healing for me and the other survivors in our meetings." I am reminded of how important it was just to acknowledge feeling out of control. It was much better than just spinning.

Jump at Shadows

jump at shadows
  turn at the touch of a breeze

shift at the slightest sound
  leave your skin at the blast of a sneeze

focus at the rustle of leaves
  feel every vibration beneath your feet

listen at the place
  where words, feelings
  and thoughts meet

hear the quality in a relationship
  by the sync of their heartbeats

belief is not required
  for every experience
life is just not that neat

jump at shadows
  turn at the touch of a breeze

look deeply into existence
  sense, search, and love without ease

Jump at Shadows MiniQuest

The Call
One day, I noticed that I was very jumpy. I jumped at every little thing.

The Quest
I decided to acknowledge what I was noticing. I spent a few minutes thinking about all the things that had made me jump on that one day. So I wrote about it.

The Return
When I return to this poem, I realize how it helped me accept those days when I was going to be jumpy for awhile. On those days, I'd have to work at living and loving life even if I was feeling uneasy.

1–10 Years

remember.....
those one through ten years
those where do I begin years
those family and friend years
those when will these end years

those learning of sin years
those keep me sane to the end years
those help me find a way to win years
those hiding where fear begins years

those deep lessons within years
those lessons learned that offend years
those lessons to the end years
those lessons that sneak in years

and here we are in these years
wondering about the then years
how they influence the now fears
why we can't believe what our ears hear

deep in the then years
were planted hidden fears
that move us to hide tears
replace them with hard sneers
fight hard *not* to see clear
holding lessons close, near
for that which we hold
is held dear

those deep lessons within years
those lessons learned to offend years
those lessons to the end years
those lessons that sneak in years
those infamous one through ten years

1-10 Years MiniQuest

The Call
I'd been reading about what researchers said childhood was *supposed* to be like. I was struck immediately about how much of what they said was nothing like what I lived through.

The Quest
As I thought about what my first ten years taught me, I just started writing and weaving thoughts together as they came to mind.

The Return
When I return to this poem, I realize I have a emotional snapshot of what my first ten years were like.

Little One

a scream caught into a smile
  on his little face
        bad men
              helping evil men
                    continue to steal
                    his innocence away
  that is how he felt
    that is what his heart told him
          what his aching body showed him
                day after day
          as the trial tripped and sputtered on
    again and again taking him
  through the injury anew
    now he is questioning
        if he will make it through
                    flashes of feelings
                        sights of that day
  smells, his smells
    the ones that won't go away
        he didn't ask for this
                though *that man* told him he had
          how could a child even know to ask
    for something like that?
  sitting in a big chair
    with his legs hanging down
          cleaned and pressed
                when jeans would have been
                        his preference
  all these strange people around
  staring, whispering
    stealing glances his way
          pretending to be looking past his face

he should have said, "No."

when the adults told him to do this
　　but he had said, "NO!" to *that man*
and then it had no imprint
he sits dreading going up
to that throne to speak
　　　　somehow he knows
　　　　　　he won't feel like a King
　　　　　　　　he won't even feel like
　　　　　　　　　　a little Prince
　　　　he hasn't felt like that since
that man laid him down to rest
　　then stole from him his innocence
　　　　　　they keep talking about justice
　　　　　　　　he's only eight now
　　　　　but this trial hasn't felt just yet
he now knows
　　this just is
　　　　day-after-day
　　　　　this just is
　　　another few days they keep saying

God make it stop he keeps praying
so he wears that little scream
caught into a smile on his face
not knowing that in a few days
the struggles won't end
it may be years before they really begin

Little One MiniQuest

The Call
In the newspaper there was a story about a little
boy who was going to have to testify at a child
sexual abuse trial.

The Quest
I tried to remember what it was like for me when I
was eight years old. Then I imagined I was sitting
in the court room looking at the young boy and
wondering what he was thinking.

The Return
When I return to this poem, I realize the courage it
would take for an eight year old to talk about being
raped. I always hope the courage it takes for
anyone to testify will be there for them during the
long years of healing ahead.

surviving

surviving

surviving

surviving

surviving

surviving

surviving

surviving

surviving

surviving

surviving

surviving

surviving

surviving

surviving

surviving

surviving

surviving

surviving

surviving

surviving

surviving

surviving

surviving

surviving

surviving

surviving

surviving

surviving

surviving

surviving

Heart Hunger

heart hunger ravishes her soul
     and licks at the corners of her deepest dreams
it spins fantasies to carry her through the day
     so rich and vivid that they are real
     at least that's how it seems
heart hunger tugs her to and fro
     tosses her life into a shambles at every turn
it breaks things to pieces before they are whole
     offering again and again lessons to learn
heart hunger seeks to be her teacher
     yet caught in a fog she turns and turns
it is patient and kind in a ruthless way
     offering over and over only lessons she's earned
heart hunger has stalked her, her whole life long
     a brutally warming rain that seems to never end
it is destined to berate and guide her
     until the current pattern of her choices
     comes to an end
     heart hunger is prepared to be her
       ever present
         constantly irritating
        always loving
         friend

Heart Hunger MiniQuest

The Call

In a Survivors of Incest Anonymous meeting, one woman's story really stuck with me. I could hear her yearning to heal.

The Quest

When I got home, it occurred to me that she was hungry to be loved, like all of us. A phrase came to mind: heart-hunger.

The Return

When I return to this poem, I realize that we all want love. Because of that, a hunger to heal stalks us; trying to push us to reconnect with the love we are all born with the right to receive.

Searching

Visions

visions, I see in my mind
flashes of light
   energy, blending in kind
forming
 transforming and
   forming again
    visions, so vivid that
      germinate within
the struggle to bring them out
 is where my work begins
visions, I see in my mind
 flashes of light
   energy blending in kind
    I sense the energy
     I feel the vibes
      they ride along my spirit
taunting my
mind
challenging, daring, ebbing through
  manifesting, regressing
   manifesting again, energy struggling too
forming, transforming
  forming again
   flashes of light
   energy blending in kind
    visions so vivid
    that dominate my mind

Visions MiniQuest

The Call
Sometimes we get flashes of things that have
happened – images from dreams, sounds we don't
understand, day dreams, buried memories.

The Quest
I wrote to capture what it is like to deal with
flashbacks, dreams, visions and unexplainable
images that just pop up out of nowhere.

The Return
When I return to this poem, I realize that the
images we see affect not just our mind, but can also
trigger our body to respond. Sometimes it causes
restlessness in our spirit and soul too.

Vibrations

I see the unseen
I speak the unspoken
silently, internally, relentlessly
it is at the heart of me
don't you see?
don't *you* see?

I hear the unheard
I feel the unfelt
silently, internally, relentlessly
it is at the heart of me
don't you hear?
don't you see?
it's a challenging way to be

    this is what I pick up
    when I just walk down the street
vibrations reaching depths and heights unknown
untouchable, unspeakable in the ways this world knows
but as natural as breath in the worlds where it flows

energy speaking a language beyond
something you sense
    without making a sound
standing in the portal
the door between
this and that
few have seen
some chaotic
and some serene
have you ever sensed an energy scream?
have you ever touched confusion's stream?

have you frolicked in the valley of doubt?
have you heard the whisper of loves first shout?
have you sensed the flow of deep knowing?
have you felt the pulse of energies growing?
have you been swept in the undertow of concern?
have you felt the heat of fear's deep burn?
vibrations reaching depths and heights unknown
untouchable, unspeakable in the ways
this world knows
but as natural as breath
in the worlds where I go

Vibrations MiniQuest

The Call
Some days we can be so sensitive it's like we pick up on the feelings of everyone we meet or pass on the street.

The Quest
I was in a meeting of other survivors and noticed that people's faces, postures, and voice tones seemed to reveal anger, confusion, and chaos as they listened to others talk. I decided to try to describe it.

The Return
When I return to this poem, I realize that reconnecting with my own emotions helps me empathize and pick up on what other people are feeling, too.

searching

searching

searching

searching

searching

searching

searching

searching

searching

searching

searching

searching

searching

searching

searching

searching

searching

searching

searching

searching

searching

searching

searching

searching

searching

searching

searching

searching

searching

searching

searching

searching

Silence

dark silence
  green silence
      blue silence
         golden silence
           red silence
              orange silence
             violet silence
             clear silence
           clean silence
         thick silence
      calm silence
   violent silence
threatening silence

who can say silence is just silence
silence is more alive
than words on most days
because it speaks truth
behind words' hazy ways

if you want to know the truth
something that always stays
listen today to what
silence has to say

Silence MiniQuest

The Call
Many times we find ourselves just sitting in silence.

The Quest
I wanted to try to explain that all silence is not the same. The emotions inside, or the thoughts, often seem to have a mood or a color.

The Return
When I return to this poem, it reveals to me many of the different moods that wash through us as we sit in silence. Silence is not always the *quiet time* people think it is.

Voices

voices in the night
voices on the wind
souls that share my journey
voices that speak in my voice
feet that have walked my journey

words
echoes
ghosts of those who went before
what about the searchers in the silence?
what about the voices in the night?

voices in the night
voices on the wind
souls that share my journey
voices that speak in my voice
feet that have walked my journey

words
echoes
ghosts of those who went before
what about the searchers in the silence?
what about the voices in the night?

Voices MiniQuest

The Call
After hearing what other people had lived through in one of the support group meetings, I would go home and think about some of the stories I had heard.

The Quest
One night I couldn't sleep. I wanted to capture what it was like to be haunted by the stories of what people do to those whom they say they love.

The Return
When I return to this poem it explains insomnia.

Untitled One

then, light dark shadow angels
now, flutter–fall–glide
there
lightly heavy on the watery air
between, before, the worlds

when I see them
will they see me?
here, we speak but don't talk
present, there, crushing-rock-feathers
far tumble down, past, upon
where, through, and within them – unseen

ever present, I feel them
ever now, they feel-me-feel
ever old, we speak but don't talk

always, energy brilliantly dull
always, fades brightly on the void between
the worlds
always, I sense them
always, they sense-me-sense
always, we speak but don't talk

light dark shadow angels
flutter–fall–glide
lightly heavy on the watery air
between the worlds

I see them
they see me
we speak but don't talk

crushing–rock–feathers
tumble down, past, upon
through and within them
I feel them
they feel–me–feel
we speak but don't talk

energy brilliantly dull
fades brightly on the void between the worlds
I sense them
they sense–me–sense
we speak but don't talk

Untitled One MiniQuest

The Call
I was sitting alone. I wasn't feeling well. I sat watching the flames in a fireplace on a cold day, feeling feverish. I was exhausted.

The Quest
The different colors of the flames, and the shadows they created in the room, made it seem like I was looking at two different dimensions at the same time. (It could have just been the fever.)

The Return
When I return to this poem, I think it sounds weird and strange. And that's exactly how it feels trying to figure out how to deal with sexual trauma: weird and strange.

searching

searching
searching
searching
searching
searching
searching
searching
searching
searching
searching
searching
searching
searching
searching
searching
searching
searching
searching
searching
searching
searching
searching
searching
searching
searching
searching
searching
searching
searching

Fighting

Risk The Dark

sometimes to see the light
you have to risk the dark
you have to walk down the alley
where the angry dog barks
stumble through the forest
to the sound of meadowlarks
slide down the cave
where worms and bats gawk
dive into the dream
that has no end and no start
forget everything that you
think makes you smart
look death in the eye
and still make your mark
sometimes to see the light
you have to risk the dark
face down your demons
in their homeland
squeeze out their lives
with your bare hands
stumble through your past
where there's no place to stand
dive into the depths of a hell
that would frighten any man
walk along the beach
and look under
every grain of sand
crawl along the floor
like an ant or Spiderman
fight every dust bunny
like a high powered fan
trying to find your truths
wherever you can

M.E. Hart

sometimes to see the light
you have to risk the dark
fear not the times when
living was stark
look in every corner
where you see dark—dark—dark
when visions in the night
froze your body made it lock
split open your soul
bleeding and in shock
wired your mind
for twisted brain locks
leaving scenes that
follow you down every block
years pass and one touch
hits you like bullets from a Glock
the light comes on
and you see life as a crock
taunting glances
and every word a mock
darkness like crows
fly and flock
since the days as a child
when soul energy locked
you see, sometimes to see the light
you have to risk the dark
and you have to go alone
because it's written in
your soul's chart
there are things in life
that-for-some are too dark
they can't go with you because
they see their face in every tree bark
they are afraid they
live under every grain of sand
where you search like an

ant or Spiderman
most can't look you in the eye
and won't shake your hand
they fear the pain and courage
that made you a real man

you see, a man who can't cry
is a boy in disguise
who puts on muscles
trying to hide
because soul blocks
as a boy made him want to die
and men can protect themselves
but for a little boy, that's a lie
so bullies and others
use little boys and make them cry
steal parts of their lives
and scar them for life
when a boy grows to be a man
this truth he must hide
it won't go away
it just festers inside
society won't help
so the man-boy must fight
he must find his own truths
and just know he's all right
face to face with his darkness
he becomes the light
you see, sometimes to see the light
you have to risk the dark
strip off the bark
silence the meadowlark
live and make your mark
even if your start was this stark
sometimes to be the light
you have to risk the dark

M.E. Hart   *Thriver's Quest* 35

Risk The Dark MiniQuest

The Call
I was looking back at all the healing work I had done over twenty years. I was remembering all the books I had read and all the stories I have heard.

The Quest
For some reason, I started looking at my healing like it was a series of quests you might read about in a book of myths. Caves, water, sand and other places came to mind.

The Return
When I return to this poem, I really like how it captures the different inner adventures I've taken to support my healing. I submitted this one for publication in the anthology, *The Journal of Healing: Wisdom From Survivors of Sexual Abuse* (2010) published by Safer Society Press.

Dark Urges

dark urges and gray matter merge
    neurons fire and chemicals surge

  memories flow like a breeze over the ocean
    traumas unfold like a quaint notion

a fading dream or a fragment from a movie
like images in the morning fog that we can
barely see

dark urges from gray matter emerge
    and in that moment memory is a curse

    images flash
      a coffin and a hearse
      the sound of Christmas carols
        streaming from the church

    the air is thick – cold and chilly
the flickering lights are much less than merry

dark urges and gray matter merge
    neurons fire and chemicals surge

  memories flow like a breeze over the ocean
    traumas unfold like a quaint notion

Dark Urges MiniQuest

The Call
Some days memories flow like a stream. This seems to be particularly true around holidays.

The Quest
I never forgot my abuse. Memories of abuse on Christmas Eve in one year flow side-by-side with all of my other memories; like the memory of going to my Grandmother's funeral on one Christmas Eve, too.

The Return
When I return to this poem, it reminds me that I have more than memories of abuse to write about. It took a while to start writing about those other things, but knowing I could use the same process helped open up other topics to me.

Synthesizing

day-after-day blushing
trembling
heart-pounding
hands-shaking
foggy-thinking
stomach-churning
muscle-tensing
hands-perspiring
brain-racing
spirit-flying
awareness-widening
heart-stretching
soul-crying
breath-sighing
psyche-spiraling
all-encompassing
daily-striving
trying
normalizing
people-denying
lonely-sighing
synthesizing
synthesizing
always synthesizing
but realizing
this is just who I am
ba-damn
ba-damn
this is just who I am
day-after-day blushing

trembling
  heart-pounding
    hands-shaking
  foggy-thinking
  stomach-churning

    muscle-tensing
    hands-perspiring
     brain-racing
     spirit-flying

awareness-widening
heart-stretching
 soul-crying
 breath-sighing
   psyche-spiraling
   all-encompassing
    daily-striving
    trying–normalizing
     people-denying
     lonely-sighing

     synthesizing–synthesizing
     always synthesizing

but realizing
this is just who I am
 ba-damn
 ba-damn
 this is just who I am

Synthesizing MiniQuest

The Call
The adrenaline that pushes my body's buttons used to go crazy on some days.

The Quest
One day, my mind seemed calm but my body kept triggering like I was being attacked. I wanted to capture what that felt like.

The Return
When I return to this poem, I remember how this used to feel. It explains how normal bodies respond when everything seems unsafe. These experiences reset our bodies. After them, normal reactions stop working normally.

fighting

fighting

fighting

fighting

fighting

fighting

fighting

fighting

fighting

fighting

fighting

fighting

fighting

fighting

fighting

fighting

fighting

fighting

fighting

fighting

fighting

fighting

fighting

fighting

fighting

fighting

fighting

fighting

fighting

fighting

Circle

when the circle was broken
something new began

when the circle was broken
something came to an end

the unbroken circle
    wound through
    the years
    through mountains
    through valleys
through anger and fear
through joys and sorrows
through happiness and tears

the unbroken circle
reaches back to the start
    a journey through time
    to the initial spark
the unbroken circle
was broken with me
    it is being repaired
        even as I speak

Circle MiniQuest

The Call
A thought circled in my mind. "Who was I born to be? How has being abused affected that?"

The Quests
I kept circling back from the present moment to the memory of the first time I was abused. I realized that something in me seemed to have been disconnected on that day and that it is fully reconnected now.

The Return
When I return to this poem, it makes me happy because it uses metaphors to describe reconnecting emotions inside with my journey in life outside. It is what healing feels like.

Illusions

his eyes were inward focused
      he spoke, struggling for the right words
and tripping over the wrong ones that
      tumbled out on their own

he couldn't believe the people in his
      world could hold a *difficulty* like that
      against him

yet, their eyes
      silently judged him
      every time he noticed them staring

"What kind of world have I fallen into?"
      a still small voice
      in the back of his head whispered

he tried to ignore it
like all the people in the room
were pretending to be ignoring him

they didn't have the strength
to take care of anyone in that
much need
and neither did he

the words *post traumatic stress*
were just too frightening to heed

so he joined them
and pretended not to need too
and together
their illusions wove a tight web of denial
that stretched easily across the room

M.E. Hart

Illusions MiniQuest

The Call
One guy in a sexual abuse meeting told the story of how his family reacted when he tried to tell them what happened to him.

The Quest
I imagined being in the room with him and seeing what he had described to us. I wrote about it when I got home.

The Return
When I return to this poem, I realize how clearly it captures what happens when someone first tries to break the *"Don't tell"* rule that sexual predators – and society – seem to impose on us. Denial is the most predictable of first responses, quickly followed by avoidance. It takes courage to break through both of them. For many, these are necessary steps to rediscovering the life they we were born to lead. Others may need support, but might never have the need to confront family members. Each healing journey is unique.

Realizing

Memories

memories that need a voice
     are of the most *patient* kind

they rest in the corners of the heart
     and worm their way into the mind

memories that need a voice
     speak through the body in signs

they run along the nerves
     like sap flowing within a vine

memories that need a voice
     hide deep like fine wine

they never fight to be first in line
     and only reveal themselves one at a time

memories that need a voice
     are of the most *patient* kind

Memories MiniQuest

The Call
After hearing hundreds of stories from men and women about sexual trauma, I noticed a trend.

The Quest
I tried to put into words how each person seems to be stalked by a particular memory of an event that wants to be dealt with in the present moment.

The Return
When I return to this poem, it holds the hope that everyone has something inside that is trying to push them to heal.

Calling Back My Spirit

I'm calling back my spirit
  and I want the world to hear it

I'll let the universe flow
    through me like a stream
    dip your hand in
    and take all you need

    but the core of my spirit belongs
    only to me

I'm calling back my spirit
    from your needs and my past
    I'll put it back together
    in this life that will be my last

I'll transform into a pillar of light
I'll live from its center for the rest of my life

I'm calling back my spirit
and I want the world to hear it
    universe flows and darkness clears it
    nothing can touch it and no one can
    steer it

I'm calling it all back
I'm calling back by spirit
and as the universe
flows through me like a stream
dip your hand in and take all you need

Calling Back My Spirit MiniQuest

The Call
Men and women often talk about *"losing something"* because of experiencing trauma. I think about that *lost thing* as a part of our core Spirit.

The Quest
I wanted to flip the *"losing something"* and turn it into *"getting it back."* A thought came to mind about calling back all parts of my Spirit and claiming ownership over them for the rest of my life.

The Return
When I return to this poem, I find it empowering. I read it often – to remember, not to forget – that healing is happening.

Life

life is in the intangibles
not the hard and fast
not in what you can have and hold
but in what will definitely pass

it's in the glance that brings a smile
connecting without words
it's in the brush of a hand
to get the attention that you deserve

it's in the warmth in your heart
when thoughts flow of the ones you love
it's in all the things you can never touch
with your hand in a velvet glove

life is in the intangibles
and there also dwells love
if you take time to learn this
breathe, hold, and live this
both life and love will offer you a very
special gift
you will know a most precious thing
you will hold life's bliss

for in the final moments
before we journey into the unknown
it's our life and loves that will bind us here
or guide us peacefully home

Life MiniQuest

The Call
Clients, colleagues, and friends were living, and dying, of complications due to AIDS.

The Quest
I was on a hospice team for a friend in his final days and the process gave me a great perspective on what's really important. So I wrote: Life.

The Return
When I return to this poem, it takes me back, and grounds me in the present moment. It shows life's unpredictability and provides a clearer focus on what's important: Love & Support.

Sometimes Angels

sometimes angels
        have got to remember to fly
especially after we think
        parts of ourselves have died
our wings get heavy
      and fold in at an awkward bend
our thoughts get
      caught in an internal whirlwind
weeks stretch to years lost in work before
we know
      and we forget to fly
      forget to let go
dust in the corners
      and things left undone
remind us every day
      of the moment we started to run
we run, walk, away from every one
      or maybe we half-heartedly try
but we never face it down
      step up to the cliff, and fly
sometimes angels
      have got to remember to fly

if we don't, we stop, we stay, we die

remember to fly
      please, a plea, a whisper, a sigh
        please remember to fly

Sometimes Angels MiniQuest

The Call
A friend of mine died from suicide.

The Quest
I had noticed a talented young man who was having troubles he wouldn't talk to anyone about. We were scheduled to begin running together on Saturday mornings. Our first run was to be the Saturday *after* he died. He never got the chance to step up to the cliff and fly. Sitting in sadness, I wrote.

The Return
When I return to this poem, it reminds me to keep moving forward, and to encourage others to do the same.

No Clowns

weather your storms
    each one as it comes

they'll help prepare
    you for the final one

no time for denial
    no time to suppress

you don't know the hour
    it's the final show – no dress

so weather your storms
    learn to face fear down

step-by-step is the best way
    on the last day
        there'll be no send in the clowns

No Clowns MiniQuest

The Call
A friend was struggling with clinical depression and doing all the right things. He was going to counselors, talking to friends, and accepted electroshock treatments. It didn't work. He became the fifth man I knew who committed suicide.

The Quest
I was angry. I was in no mood to be metaphorical or lyrical. So I wrote this plain truth poem in the voice of a cold universe.

The Return
When I return to this poem, it reminds me of the simple truth, that with life comes death. No one gets out alive, and weathering the storms the best we can is what we are all called to do.

Healing

Healing Walks

darkness denied
lives a reckless life
darkness denied
creates pain and strife
darkness denied
lives the seven deadly sins
then goes back to the beginning and lives
them again
darkness denied takes over a life
uses up its energy
and slips off into the night
why would we choose darkness denied?
because it's the perfect place
for wounded spirits to hide
      and, healing walks
      it does not run
   it rises slowly with the morning sun
   floats lightly on the morning breeze
whispers its mantra
through the rustling trees
healing walks with the shimmering brook
flowing over mountains
through winding crooks
crooks and crannies
    twists and turns
    healing walks
      it does not yearn
      the trees and flowers drink it in
   and then quietly breathe it out again
it floats on the breath that each plant makes
riding the air that we will soon take
healing walks through us

as we take it in
in some it will rest
in some it will end
and with a heat of blazing fire
healing comforts and warms
holding life gently in loving arms

healing walks
it does not swoon
even in the light of
the blue full moon

it rides the waves of
the blue moon beams
it travels freely
where each beam gleams
healing walks
it does not run, it travels the path with
moon and sun
wind and fire
snow and rain
healing walks without shame
unafraid in the face of love
unafraid of a caring hug
unafraid of pain and bliss
healing walks, softly
like a gentle kiss
walk with open mind and heart
you don't want to miss this

Healing Walks MiniQuest

The Call
At some point in my healing, denying and disassociating stopped working in a helpful way and only allowed darkness to grow. I was forced to try other things. I found this to be true for other survivors, too.

The Quest
After realizing that denying and disassociating were not working, but instead were allowing darkness to grow; I flipped the script, and focused on the slow, natural process of healing that we notice when we let nature be our guide. Slowing down, walking, watching how the seasons change helps us get a different perspective.

The Return
When I return to this poem, it takes me on a mental journey that soothes my emotions and returns my body to balance.

healing

healing

healing

healing

healing

healing

healing

healing

healing

healing

healing

healing

healing

healing

healing

healing

healing

healing

healing

healing

healing

healing

healing

healing

healing

healing

healing

healing

healing

Clean Slate

from high in the sky
    just above the river
two strips of life
    lie parallel on the water –

one a bright, new, lime green
    the other a dust brown
both, floating on the water
    like fluffy down

from high in the sky
    just above the river
two eagles circle
in a dance over the water –

one swoops and circles low
    with a sharp eye on the green
one climbs and angles high
    eyeing the brown

in the blink of an eye they've disappeared
    and so has the down –
the placid water ripples clear and clean
    and off in the distance
    a new earth can be seen

M.E. Hart

Clean Slate MiniQuest

The Call
I was walking home from work one day and saw
two hawks circling in the sky.

The Quest
I sat down in a park and changed the hawks to
eagles and started writing about how the darkness
of life must be balanced with the lightness in life
for us to heal.

The Return
When I return to this poem, it reminds me that we
are always recreating our *"new earth"* a little
everyday. The journey continues.

Be True

be true to who you are
     live your passion

love your life
     share your soul

teach what you know
     we have what we gave
     a wise person said

what do you have to give?

     the honesty in our souls
     seeps, twists, rumbles, and flows

our intents and actions
cause consequences
     that live in the world
     long after we go

be true to who you are
     share your soul

give all that you have to give
and the ripples you leave behind

     will only continue to grow

M.E. Hart

Be True MiniQuest

The Call
Traumas throw our life off course. After them, we begin to question: What is true? Who are we? How have we been changed? Even if you thought you had yourself figured out, after the trauma, all understanding is out the window.

The Quest
I sat down and began to write a poetic note to – Self. Something took over and an *Inside Guide* started writing about the lesson I had learned without even realizing it: Only we get to define who we *really are!*

The Return
When I return to this poem, it reads like a Life Vision Statement for my healing journey. Be true. Live passion. Love life. Share soul. Teach – Know.

Truth Teller

when the truth will set you free
  then a truth teller
  is all you can be

when nights are dark
  and sleep won't come

when memories leave you
  no where to run

then there is only one thing
  left to be done

yes, it'll be hard
  no, it won't be fun

and nobody else can do it
  because you are the one

you see
when the truth will set you free
then a truth teller is all you can be

and, you don't have to tell your truth to me
there's only one person who has the need
  to hear the truth
  feel the truth
  deeply and clearly

doing the work that needs to be done
talking the talk of the crazy one

knowing that the freedom of sleep
        someday will come
and when it does
        you will have won

when the truth will set you free
        then a truth teller
        is all you can be

it's all about
what you've lived through

and that's what you've got to do
        crawl back to the honesty
        that has always been you

look it in the eye
dare it to fight
speak it just as it was
and just know you're all right

when being a truth teller
        will set you free
        then a truth teller
        is all you can be

Truth Teller MiniQuest

The Call
I kept hearing people say, *"It's always best to tell the truth."* I reflected on all the reasons you have to be careful about doing that when dealing with sexual trauma.

The Quest
I saw how important it was for me – and the men and women whose stories I have heard – to be honest with ourselves first and foremost. Even if we chose to never speak to another person about it. It was important to acknowledge, "Yes this happened to me." But not necessarily always safe, or wise, to tell everybody about it.

The Return
When I return to this poem, it reminds me to keep being truthful to myself about all aspects of my relationships with others. Much of it remains inside, but it is always acknowledged by me, for me. Some of us need that.

healing

healing

healing

healing

healing

healing

healing

healing

healing

healing

healing

healing

healing

healing

healing

healing

healing

healing

healing

healing

healing

healing

healing

healing

healing

healing

healing

healing

healing

healing

healing

healing

Wisdom's Past

through the gray darkness
  through the godless hell
       through the rain of tears
       through don't tell, don't tell

through endless fears
  over the razor's edge
       through suicide's garden
           this I pledge
to know my love
  as deep as my anger
to stare into the eyes of darkness
  face-to-face with danger
to understand the causes
  of all of my fears
to uproot, slash and burn that
  soul-wrenching terrain clear

to search deeper than the surface
  when life's triggers appear
to go beyond understanding
when someone I love has been smeared

to stand tall and not flinch
  when daily bias pricks my
skin again and again
  to never question the truth
  my heart tells
even when friends
  don't hear my truth–well

to reclaim all stolen parts of me
to spend my life
  every second I have left free

free from patterns
  that steal my joy

free from the hatred
  in the eyes that
silently call me "boy"

free from the chains
  media images
  re-make
free from it all
  this freedom
  I now know
  I must take

I learned hard-knock
  lessons in the gray darkness
I learned of life's evil
  living through the godless hell
I learned of life's pain
  through the rain of tears
I learned of the terror in silence
  through don't tell, don't tell
I learned of lost strength
  facing the endless fears
I learned delicate balance
  walking over the razor's edge
I learned there's no pain worth
walking back
through suicide's garden
these are lesson's of wisdom's past
I intend to live them now
hard and fast

Wisdom's Past MiniQuest

The Call
One day my whole healing journey washed over me
and triggered strong emotions.

The Quest
I mentally surfed the emotions and tried to tack
words to them. One part of this poem was
confirmed by a hand survey showing that many of
the 200 men attending the 2010 Oprah shows had
contemplated suicide at one time on their healing
journey.

The Return
When I return to this poem, it is a concise reminder
of what I've lived through. It reminds me to keep
living what I've learned one day at a time.

healing

healing

healing

healing

healing

healing

healing

healing

healing

healing

healing

healing

healing

healing

healing

healing

healing

healing

healing

healing

healing

healing

healing

healing

healing

healing

healing

healing

healing

healing

healing

healing

healing

Thriving

Heartbeat

the sound of your heartbeat
    is the only cadence
        that can put me to sleep

the light in your eyes
    each morning is the sun
        that helps me wake

when the storms of stress shake me off
course
    the memory of my sleeping
        and waking lifts my remorse

I am not all that I want to be
    but I definitely am a better me
    when I am spending life with you

Heartbeat MiniQuest

The Call
I was remembering the first time I fell asleep with my head resting on someone's chest.

The Quest
I never thought I would be able to trust anyone to sleep in their presence, let alone sleep in the same room. Looking back triggered the sound that grounded me: the sound of a heartbeat.

The Return
When I return to this poem, it reminds me of the power one personal connection has to change your life forever.

I Love You

I love you
    heart
    mind
    spirit
    body and
    soul
when I first saw you
my heart skipped a beat
then it skipped another
trying to get back in sync
when it finally found a rhythm to rest into
one that felt natural and full of peace
it was beating to the rhythm of yours, and to
my surprise our hearts were in sync
when we first met my mind went fuzzy
as we continued to talk it started to clear
as I listened to what life had done to you
I noticed our journeys were very different –
yet
our lessons were similar
and our hopes and dreams
flowed down the same stream
when I first meditated
beside the ocean with you
I thought you would think me strange

yet, I let my spirit relax

and breathed in real deep

the ocean breeze filled me

and I felt tension release

after the meditation our spirits were

      swirling together with ease

when I first felt your touch

my body started to sing a strange song

I buzzed from the inside out

I couldn't recognize the key and when you

touched me again

your energy joined in and it made

a new kind of harmony

when my life's energy

began to swirl in a new way

I couldn't help but notice that it was

because of you

I was confused by the changes

but parts of me felt finally awake and totally

brand new

I knew I wanted to continue to live this way

and that's why I love you

         heart

         mind

         spirit

         body and

         soul

         every day

I Love You MiniQuest

The Call
Feelings of love struck like lightening and I didn't know what it was or what to do about it. Life had not prepared me for this.

The Quest
The weekend love entered my life, I fell into a whole of healing light as deep as the hole of darkness I was trying to climb out of. Only looking back now do I realize this. At the time it was something my mind never thought would happen and my heart was surprised and frightened to feel.

The Return
When I return to this poem, it reminds me how close I came to missing out on one of life's most sacred gifts: loving relationships. Abuse and trauma should not be allowed to do that, but all too often, that is the result for some people. We must always remember that as long as there is breath in our bodies healing is possible.

thriving

thriving

thriving

thriving

thriving

thriving

thriving

thriving

thriving

thriving

thriving

thriving

thriving

thriving

thriving

thriving

thriving

thriving

thriving

thriving

thriving

thriving

thriving

thriving

thriving

thriving

thriving

thriving

thriving

thriving

thriving

thriving

thriving

thriving

thriving

Spiritual Partnership

are you willing to share all of my smiles and cries?
    or will you only take the smiles
    and with cries close your ears and hide your eyes?
do you think you could be my soft place to fall
when the world seeks to suck every drop of my hope
    every drop, tries to take it all?
or will you only be there when I stand tall
    turning to walk away when you sense a flinch
    forcing me to call?

will you float on my laughter?
    will you bathe in my tears
    putting them to some use
    washing away the pain of years
    washing away undeserved fears
    healing them, transforming them, clearing them
    and releasing them all right now, right here?
or will you flee
    at tears' first glimmer in the corner of my eye
showing me it's not okay to share my pain
    it's not okay to cry?

will you be my spiritual training ground
    the safe place for me to grow
so that on my final day on this planet
    I will know – really know –
    that I have been loved?

I know these are a lot of questions, but I just need the answer to
one – will you share all of my smiles and cries, so that I might
be fully alive every day for the rest of my life? will you love me?
will you be mine eternally from this night?

M.E. Hart

Spiritual Partnership MiniQuest

The Call
My best friend had introduced me to the woman he was going to marry.

The Quest
He asked me to officiate his wedding, rather than be his Best Man. In the year leading up to it, we talked about the great qualities of their relationship. I wrote this poem for their wedding.

The Return
When I return to this poem, I realize how it reflects what I feel in my relationship too. It makes me wonder if some aspects of this poem have universal appeal. We all yearn to be loved, and struggle to find what that means in a complex world where none of us are perfect.

I'm Not Sure You Know

I'm not sure you know this
    because I've never said it out loud
you are my hope for humanity
    the one who defines the crowd

your laughter lifts
    the burdens from my life
your easy ways of treading the earth
    my example, in the strife

you carry what you've been given
    with a simple kind of grace
it shines light into the darkness
    brings peace and inspiration
    to every living space

I marvel at your patience
    and the energy you create
in the simplest moments of the day
    you connect in every way
    is this something you can teach
    something one can learn
    or just something you are born with
    that another can't earn?

I'm not sure you know this
    because I've never said it out loud
    you are my hope for humanity
    the one who stands out in the crowd

I'm Not Sure You Know MiniQuest

The Call
I realized that I keep a lot of nice thoughts about
people inside my head and don't always say them
out loud.

The Quest
I thought I should write out what I wanted to say to
my own Spiritual Partner.

The Return
When I return to this poem, it reminds me that I
have a life saving partner in healing and thriving.

Silent Thrivers

there is a tribe of silent thrivers
that many people don't know

they carry wounds that cut into
the depths of their very souls

they have survived unspeakable
horrors many would not believe

especially if they saw the
absolutely normal and
successful lives they lead

they hold a human potential
we should all have access to

a resilience that heals the worst
humans can live through

childhood rape, attempted soul murder
and deep psychological abuse

words, that for most people
would have no use

those in the silent tribe
would wish for that too

that healing from these traumas
was something they did not have to do

but having taken that courageous journey
to create and find amazing lives

they wonder why society holds them in a
shame so deep that they still have to hide

humanity is in great need of the healing
wisdom that this tribe of silent thrivers
must quietly hold
yes, there is a tribe of silent thrivers that the
world
would do well to come to know

how they survived
how they live now
how they grew to thrive

this exceptionally large
     enigmatic
     unique
     and all too human tribe

whose identities they still feel
     they must hide

Silent Thrivers MiniQuest

The Call
Sitting in the audience of the Oprah Winfrey Show
with 200 Courageous Men – survivors of sexual
trauma – and some of their partners, I was moved
by how few stories of thriving were told.

The Quest
I know many men and women who are getting up,
fixing breakfast for their children, taking them to
school, going to work and living life after surviving
sexual trauma. They have no need to speak
publicly but they thrive in their private lives.
Someone must honor their stories.

The Return
When I return to this poem, it reminds me that it is
a natural state of being human for us to strive to
heal after trauma. Resilience is wired into who we
are. Sometimes we discover it before it's too late.
Sometimes, we don't. Every life is touched by the
choices we make.

Bonus Poems

for your thriver's quest

Childhood

childhood, remember?
one through ten, who you were then?
all you have been?

Broken Hearts

broken hearts still beat
they skip from time to time though
finding new rhythms

Mystery

full of mystery
accidents happen in life
And we walk away

Ancestry

there is this energy
in our ancestry
that shows the light
and the dark
that rides with our breath
and flows in our blood
and the quickest way
to access it is through love

Dark Shadows

I was raised in dark shadows
    and tossed in silent streams

I listened deeply into sleepless nights
    and lost track of all of my dreams

I saw through a child's eyes
    things no child should see

my body carries memories
that should never have been forced on me

I struggled through life's trials
    with ripped and torn identities

I searched each religion
    to find a God who would set me free

I found what I was searching for
    in the beats of my own heart

Beat-by-beat guiding me back
to the love that belonged to me at life's start

Creaks of the floor

once upon a midnight dreary
while I slumbered, weak and weary
from living events of life the day before
suddenly, I heard a tapping
or was it bare feet slapping across the floor?

ah, clearly now I remember
it was deep in dark December
and every step was marked by a creak of the floor
every step was marked with a creak of the floor

eagerly, I sought to burrow
into sleep to burrow
so that I could not hear creaks of the floor
but I heard the creaks and nothing more

tis some visitor, I queried
creaking across the floor
some late visitor?
it must be a dream and nothing more
it must be a dream, these creaks of the floor
a slight movement did I make
shifting a little for comforts sake
and listening harder to see if I could hear more
silence I heard, no creaks of the floor

M.E. Hart

silence I heard, and nothing more

as I drifted, nearly falling

faintly I heard a cricket's calling

at least I thought it was a cricket

it was so far away, somewhere outside the door

it must have been a cricket and nothing more

the wings of sleep had deeply embraced me

what I heard was just a trace you see

for weary and worn, sleep had encased me

and sights and faint sounds didn't matter anymore

only sleep was important, only sleep

and nothing more

suddenly the beast was upon me

with a silent swiftness it was upon me

my movement was restrained

by the weight it bore

it must be a nightmare and nothing more

reluctantly, I tried to gather up my senses

to further explore

though sleep was all I wanted

rest and nothing more

feeling the weight of flesh on bone

feeling the breath of life my lungs bore

I climbed out of sleep hoping to explore

to find myself in a dream and nothing more

I wanted to erase the dream and nothing more

but when my senses were re-awakened

and they climbed to the end of my flesh

I was shaken

flesh didn't end

there was more

I felt more flesh than my body could bear

there was more flesh and something else there

suddenly shocked into a realization

I was a aware of a violation

in the space where I'd lain down to rest

there was a violation in the space

where I had lain down to rest

another person was my best guess

when I opened my mouth to speak

breath caught in my throat

and out came a squeak

because at that moment there was a pain deep within me

a white hot flash of pain

that caused a breach deep within me

a breach through which my soul could leave

I was stunned at the sudden loss

without my soul I lie there lost

an empty vessel trapped under flesh

I was only a body trapped beneath flesh
in the place where I'd lain down to rest
I convinced myself it was a dream
and into darkness I fled with a silent scream

into darkness to wander in search of a door
I wanted out, and nothing more
I needed to find a way out of the darkness
I needed a door
I had just lain down to sleep, nothing more

years would pass, as that vessel grew
people watched and no one knew
that it carried a hole where the soul was before
nothing could fill it year after year
emotions tried, anger, hatred, loneliness, fear
there stayed a hole where the soul was before
there, there was a hole and nothing more

now the vessel is fully grown
and sinew muscle and bone have all been replaced from before
but memory, now vivid, senses ever sharp
    from years of searching to get out of the dark
        recall the night with the greatest of ease
        that the soul, now returned, was violently released

Events Live

events live inside of us

until we make peace with them

some cycle around to visit

again and again

in a room with a billion triggers

we meet one at every turn

each offering a memory

some life lesson we need to learn

lessons that come in patterns

or lessons one at a time

some deeply etched in the neurons

at the bottom of our minds

events live inside of us, some bad and many very good

some we hold onto way too long

some we let go of like we should

experiences that have served their purpose

should be released to time

those not released completely find a secret place to hide

in the color of the sunlight that dances on the wall

in the sound of that barking dog each time the owner calls

in the darkness that descends when we seek to rest our eyes

the energy that circles around us carries the stories of our lives

events live inside of us until we make peace with them

some cycle around to visit again and again

M.E. Hart

Ghost

what is a ghost
but a loving wind
that people don't understand

what is love
but an endless energy
that cycles to infinity

what is trust
but a fragile flame
once extinguished never the same

what is bliss
but a flowing stream
riding the wave of a moon beam

what is life
but a deep mystery
whose essence we may never see

whose meaning
we only learn
when death sets us free

The Listener

listening deep to the flow
    of the undertow
I hear so many things
    people don't want me to know
"Oh, I'm afraid – Oh, I'm alone – No, I can't do this on my own."
    silent fears we don't want known
        from the gift that comes
once listening skills have grown
        listening close, core of heart deep
I sense an abiding need to weep
    why, when I listen to so many lives
do I find that people have so much to hide?
    what can I do?
    what can I say
    to help people move
    from such a dark place?
    shhhh...listen....

Collection of Stories

I once wrote a collection of stories

that very few could read

they were true stories too

so that really surprised me

one person said, *"They are just too sad."*

another read a few chapters, stopped,

and then set down the book

and when I asked for it to be returned

she couldn't remember where to look

one friend said, *"We lose it on purpose,*

it's just too hard to read."

and this is from people who love me

the only ones, those stories, I would allow to read

and as I said earlier, they are stories that are true

they happened in the world I knew

they happened to someone they know too

I once wrote a collection of stories that very few could read

those very stories

form the fabric of this life that I lead

they formed the basis of my childhood

the rushing river of my adolescence

the turbulence of early adulthood

and they form the foundations of my greatest gifts

sometimes when you write stories

that very few can read

the lessons that they teach

must remain pressed in the pages like dried leaves

for they have served their purpose

if they are never seen again

they were written to heal your soul

and after all

isn't that what you wanted in the end?

I once wrote a collection of stories

that very few could read

and once, that hurt deeply

now, I find that it's just fine with me

Imagine

imagine that in your darkest hour
    in your hour of need
someone was there
    to give you great advice to heed
not diamonds or gold
    simple things
like access to food and clothes
    not a handout
        an opportunity
a chance to be free
    to discover who you were born to be
a chance to reconnect with humanity

imagine that in your darkest hour
    in your hour of need
someone was there to give you
    caring, healing, loving advice to heed

now, imagine, they were not

Poetic Madness

I use poetic madness to release my sadness

sometimes to share my gladness

to bring peace to my madness

to compensate for my badness

  yes, I must use poetic madness

  to search through my pastness

  to live in my presentness

poetic is the only way to dance with this mess

have you gotten to that point yet?

when you search for words to explain this shit

to cover pain that is bottomless

to climb out of the depths of some pit

  when you reach for clearness

  pray for nearness

  show a face that's fearless

  posture like you could care less

when you only want to return

to your first month's bliss

  years before you knew you yet?

  wouldn't you use poetic madness

  work hard to just try this – find some way,
anyway, to release pent up shit?

  I use poetic madness to release my sadness

  to sometimes show my gladness

  to compensate for my badness

to balance the shadow with the light

to bring what is wrong and what is right

to fight with all of my might

to face up to my strife

I use poetic madness – to save my life!

Stream of Stories

can you hear the stream of stories
    that flow in the river of your life?

can you smell the stench in the darkness
    that causes pain and strife?

can you sense the presence
    in a moment pregnant with new light?

can you see the visions in the stories
    that flow in the river of life?

can you feel the vibrations
that ripple from the darkness to the light?

can you let the stream flow
    as easily as flight?

will you flow with the stories
    that stream in the river of life?

will you fly with the visions
    that come both day and night?

M.E. Hart

will you look deeply without fear
    into moments of delight?

will you give yourself a chance
    to learn how to spiritually fight?

will you walk through your struggles
    holding on with all your might?

can you, will you, flow with the stream
    of stories in the river of life?

will you explore with me
    until we both dissolve into light?

200 Courageous Men

I was one of 200 courageous men
in the audience of two ground breaking
Oprah Winfrey shows
to break the silence on a secret
that the world already knows

little boys are sexually abused
and grow to be uneasy men
one in six statistics say
so what happens to all of them?

200 came to the the Oprah shows
millions more abused did not go
when I watched those shows on my
TV screen
some small part of me was glad
 that I could not be clearly seen

those feelings troubled me
they tormented my soul
did some secret part me
not really want the world to know?
so I had a talk with the me
that I had been
and asked
what these troubling feelings
were all about then
this is what he said to my surprise:
"yes, I wanted to go,
I just wanted some stories from my side.
where were the Thrivers
who lived through it and are living well?

why did they only show what it was like
down in the depths of hell?
where were the happy fathers
who live healed from their pain?
who love their children deeply
who are proud that their children
will not carry their shame?
where were the strategies
that kept them all alive?
especially after so many admitted
that at one time they wanted to die?
where were the doctors and lawyers
clerks and sanitation engineers
who can smile and laugh
and live now without fear?"

don't get me wrong
I think the shows did some good
some stories were told
but there were other stories that should
have had more than one segment
one segment of smiles
one segment of strength
one segment of hope
one segment of this is how you cope

I was one the 200 courageous men on the
ground breaking Oprah Winfrey shows
yes, I'm glad I went
I'm not ashamed if people know
but, I was still disappointed
at what they didn't show
so, I guess they left that part
for you and me
we have to tell
the rest of the story

thriving
thriving
thriving
thriving
thriving
thriving
thriving
thriving

thriving
thriving
thriving
thriving
thriving
thriving
thriving
thriving
thriving
thriving
thriving
thriving
thriving
thriving
thriving
thriving
thriving
thriving
thriving
thriving
thriving

About the Author

M.E. Hart, or Hart as he prefers to be called, draws upon his healing journey and diverse life experiences in developing his poems. He is an attorney, actor, scriptwriter, poet, and certified executive coach.

Hart received his BA in Russian Language and Literature and his JD from the University of Kentucky. He also completed the Senior Executive Leadership Certificate Program at Georgetown University.

Hart's legal career began at the DC Office of Human Rights where he served as Legal Advisor to the Director and worked on the frontlines of the AIDS epidemic, investigating, mediating, and educating about AIDS discrimination.

He left that position to explore the hidden passion of acting. He auditioned and was accepted into the acting company of Washington's renowned Arena Stage. For six seasons he performed in a wide variety of dramas, musicals, and cutting-edge experimental theater.

Pivoting back to the law, Hart became an Attorney/Producer at the Federal Judicial Center, where he produced multimedia programming. His duties included educating new federal judges and the position gave him the honor of working directly with the Chief Justice of the Supreme Court.

He then moved into the business world, adapting his acting talents to train management professionals with dramatic vignettes and improvisation.

As CEO of Hart Learning Group, Hart leads a team that helps organizations create inclusive and innovative cultures. Hart's career has taken him into Fortune 100 companies across the US, and to Belgium, Moscow, Ukraine and other interesting parts of the world.

Along the way, Hart also contributed to the news journal *Moving Forward: A Journal for Survivors of Sexual Abuse and Those Who Care About Them.* His script about sexual abuse, *Family Secrets,* for the television series *In Our Lives,* earned him a National Parent's Choice Award.

His essay, *A Person Of Color Overcoming The Barriers to Group Participation,* appears in the book *Leaping Upon the Mountains,* by psychotherapist Mike Lew.

Some of his poems appear in a literary anthology, *The Journey of Healing: Wisdom from Survivors of Sexual Abuse* published by Safer Society Press. He also won the Washington D.C. Rape Crisis Center's 2010 Sexual Assault Awareness Month Poetry Slam.

Hart was proud to stand with 200 other male survivors in the final season of the Oprah Winfrey Show. That experience motivated him to devote more time to supporting men and women working to heal from unwanted sexual experiences in their lives.

He is a member of the Rape, Abuse and Incest National Network (RAINN) speakers bureau and provides inspirational keynotes and workshops at conferences across the United States. He recently shared his story with the Bristlecone Project at 1in6.org.

Today, through his poetry, workshops, and speaking engagements, Hart works to help prevent child sexual abuse and to provide hope and inspiration to people who have experienced it.

Acknowledgements

Thank you to my family, Vicki, Donna, Johnny, Tony, Alice, Mary, Baby, Nannie, Sharon, Nikki, Brandyon, Brooke, Valerie, Cameron, Maurice, Dan, Giselle, Kent, Nancy, Jerry, and Donna. Some of you are on earth and some in spirit. And thanks to those whose names are not here, but supported me in spirit but felt they couldn't say it out loud. I respect that too. Your love and support have lifted me up during the tough times.

Thank you to the 200 Courageous men, and those who love them, who attended the Oprah Shows in 2010. Being among you inspired me, motivated me, and gave me a call to action.

Special thanks to Oprah Winfrey, her staff, and Tyler Perry for making the show possible. Thank you to Dr. Maya Angelou!

Thank you to the courageous men at Mike Lew's retreat in Pennsylvania. It was great sharing healing with you.

Thank you to Bev Smith, and the team on her BET program, Our Voices. Thanks to the two other men who stood with me on that show.

Thanks to the many men and women who attend the Survivors of Incest Anonymous (SIA) meetings with me during the early 1990s. Your example of healing and living from meeting to meeting helped show me the way.

To these special people on my journey of living, learning, and healing, Marsha, Matt, Chuck, Colin, Brian, Jennell, Barry, Shaira, Giselle, Shannon, Christi, Amy, David, Dotsy, Christi, Krista, June, Frank, Pam, Robert and Ellen.

Special thanks to Bill Kane and Library Partners Press, you rock!

To the many working on the frontlines providing support to men, women, and children, I thank you:

Indira Hernard, David Lisak, Eric Stiles, Ellen Thurby, Regina Marscheider, Peter Woodbury, Santa Molina Marshall, Trina Greer, Chelsea Bro, Mike Lew, Thom Harrigan, Michelle Brickley, Bea Hanson, Dayanara Marta, Tandra Lagrone, Steve LePore, Tabatha Bennett, Lara Reyes, Pete Pollard, Neil Irvin, Delilah Rumburg, Anita Rhind, Shawn Ricks, Richard Hoffman, and Robert Miller.

A very special thanks to my readers and reviewers, Donna, Vicki, Indira, MJ, Mike, Shawn, Ellen, and Monique.

Thanks to these resources for being sources of information:

The Office on Violence Against Women, Department of Justice (OVW)

https://www.justice.gov/ovw

Casa de Esperanza

https://casadeesperanza.org

In Our Own Voices, Inc. (IOOV)

http://inourownvoices.org

The New Mexico Crime Victims Reparation Commission (CVRC)

https://www.cvrc.state.nm.us

National Council of Juvenile and Family Court Judges (NCJFCJ)

http://www.ncjfcj.org

The National Sexual Violence Resource Center (NSVRC)

https://www.nsvrc.org

DC Rape Crisis Center

http://dcrcc.org

1in6

https://1in6.org

Men Can Stop Rape

https://www.mencanstoprape.org

Pennsylvania Coalition Against Rape

http://www.pcar.org

Rape And Incest National Network

https://www.rainn.org

Stop Abuse

https://stopabuse.com

And there are many more, you can find those in your area by searching locally.

Thanks to everyone who has touched my life and brought insights through the surviving, searching, and fighting times. Those moments were where my deepest healing happened.

Thanks for your beautiful cover design MJ Vilardi, and for all you mean to my life on a daily basis.

thriving

thriving

thriving

thriving

thriving

thriving

thriving

thriving

thriving

thriving

thriving

thriving

thriving

thriving

thriving

thriving

thriving

thriving

thriving

thriving

thriving

thriving

thriving

thriving

thriving

thriving

thriving

thriving

thriving

thriving

thriving

thriving

thriving

thriving

thriving

thriving

thriving

thriving

thriving

thriving

thriving

thriving

thriving

thriving

thriving

thriving

thriving

thriving

thriving

thriving

thriving

thriving

thriving

thriving

thriving

thriving

thriving

thriving

thriving

thriving

thriving

thriving

thriving

thriving

thriving

thriving

thriving

thriving

thriving

thriving

thriving

thriving

thriving

thriving

thriving

thriving

thriving

thriving

thriving

thriving

thriving

thriving

thriving

thriving

thriving

thriving

thriving

22878725R00074

Made in the USA
Columbia, SC
05 August 2018